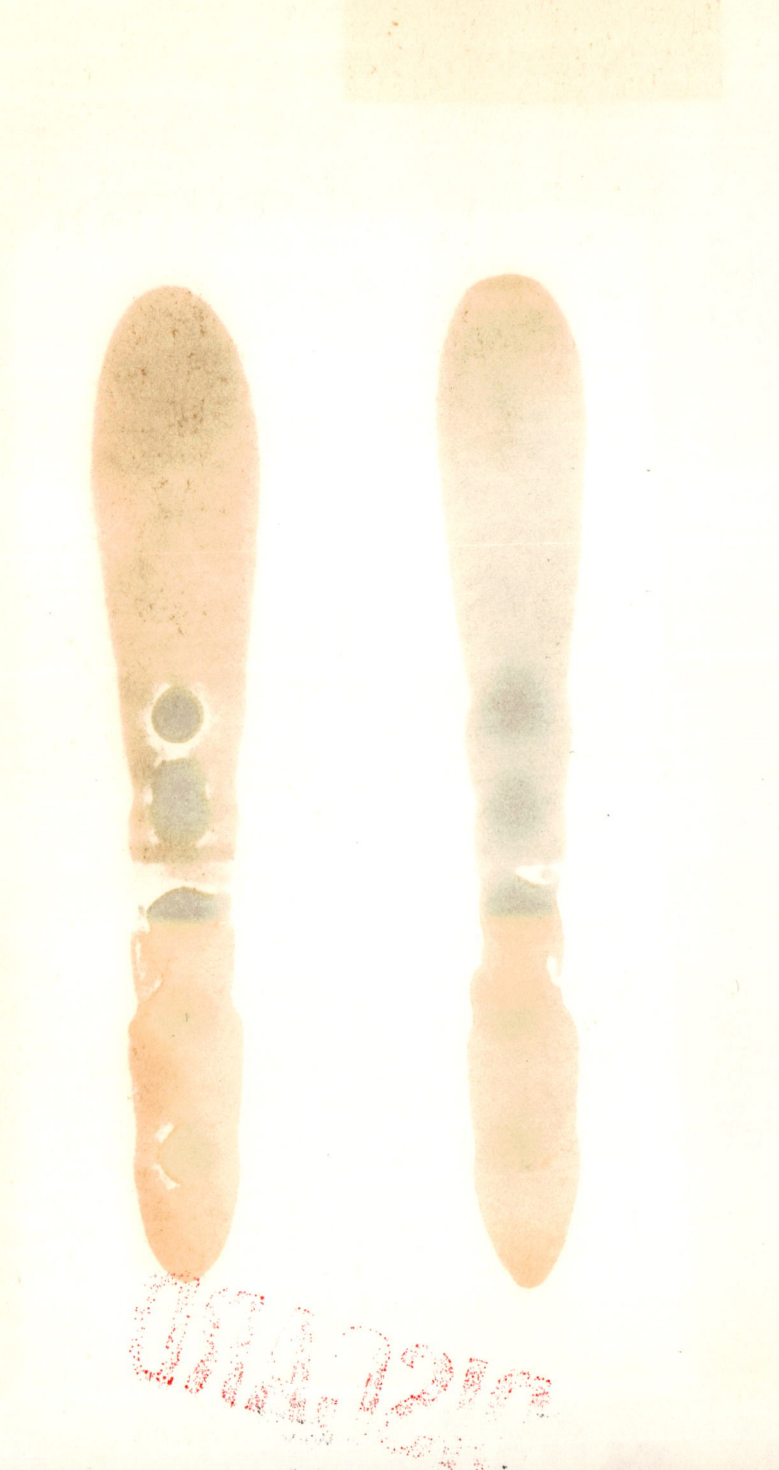

CALIFORNIA
NATIVE AMERICAN TRIBES

KAROK TRIBE

by
Mary Null Boulé

Illustrated by
Daniel Liddell

Merryant Publishing
Vashon, Washington

Book Number Eight in a series of twenty-six

1

This series is dedicated to Virginia Harding, whose editing expertise and friendship brought this project to fruition.

ISBN: 1-877599-32-8

Copyright © 1992, Merryant Publishing

7615 S.W. 257th St., Vashon, WA 98070.

FOREWORD

Native American people of the United States are often living their lives away from major cities and away from what we call the mainstream of life. It is, then, interesting to learn of the important part these remote tribal members play in our everyday lives.

More than 60% of our foods come from the ancient Native American's diet. Farming methods of today also can be traced back to how tribal women grew crops of corn and grain. Many of our present day ideas of democracy have been taken from tribal governments. Even some 1,500 Native American words are found in our English language today.

Fur traders bought furs from tribal hunters for small amounts of money, sold them to Europeans and Asians for a great deal of money, and became rich. Using their money to buy land and to build office buildings, some traders started business corporations which are now the base of our country's economy.

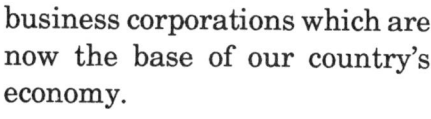

There has never been enough credit given to these early Americans who took such good care of our country when it was still in their care. The time has come to realize tribal contributions to our society today and to give Native Americans not only the credit, but the respect due them.

Mary Boulé

A-frame cradle for girls; tule matting. Tubatulabal tribe.

3

GENERAL INFORMATION

Out of Asia, many thousands of years ago, came Wanderers. Some historians think they were the first people to set foot on our western hemisphere. These Wanderers had walked, step by step, onto our part of the earth while hunting and gathering food. They probably never even knew they had moved from one continent to another as they made their way across a land bridge, a narrow strip of land between Siberia and what is now Russia, and the state of Alaska.

Historians do not know exactly how long ago the Wanderers might have crossed the land bridge. Some of them say 35,000 years ago. What historians do know is that these people slowly moved down onto land that we now call the United States of America. Today it would be very hard to follow their footsteps, for the land bridge has been covered with sea water since the thawing of the ice age.

Those Wanderers who made their way to California were very lucky, indeed. California was a land with good weather most of the year and was filled with plenty of plant and animal foods for them to eat.

The Wanderers who became California's Native Americans did not organize into large tribes like the rest of the North American tribes. Instead, they divided into groups, or tribelets, sometimes having as many as 250 people. A tribelet could number as few as three, to as many as thirty villages located close to each other. Some tribelets had only one chief, a leader who lived in the largest village. Many tribes had a chief for each village. Some leaders had no real power but were thought to be wise. Tribal members always listened with respect to what their chief had to say.

From 20 to 100 people could be living in one village, which usually had several houses. In most cases, these groups of people were related to each other. From five to ten people of one family lived in one house. For instance, a mother, a father, two or three children, a grandmother, or aunt or daughter-in-law might live together.

Village members together would own the land important to them for their well-being. Their land might include oak trees with precious acorns, streams and rivers, and plants which were good to eat. Streams and rivers were especially important to a tribe's quality of life. Water drew animals to it; that meant more food for the tribe to eat. Fish were a good source of food, and traveling by boat was often easier than walking long distances. Water was needed in every part of tribal life.

Village and tribelet land was carefully guarded. Each group knew exactly where the boundaries of its land were found. Boundaries were known by landmarks such as mountains or rivers, or they might also be marked by poles planted in the ground. Some boundary lines were marked by rocks, or by objects placed there by tribal members. The size of a territory had to be large enough to supply food to every person living there.

The California tribes spoke many languages. sometimes villages close together even had a problem understanding one another. This meant that each group had to be sure of the boundaries of other tribes around them when gathering food. It would not be wise to go against the boundaries and the customs of neighbors. The Native Americans found if they respected the boundaries of their neighbors, not so many wars had to be fought. California tribes, in spite of all their differences, were not as warlike as other tribes in our country.

Not only did the California tribes speak different languages, but their members also differed in size. Some tribes were very tall, almost six feet tall. The shortest people came from the Yuki tribe which had territory in what is now Mendocino County. They measured only about 5'2" tall. All Native Americans, regardless of size, had strong, straight black hair and dark brown eyes.

TRADE

Trading between tribes was an important part of life. Inland tribes had large animal hides that coastal tribes wanted. By trading the hides to coastal groups, inland tribes would receive fish and shells, which they in turn wanted. Coastal tribes also wanted minerals and rocks mined in the mountains by inland tribes. Obisdian rock from the northern mountains was especially wanted for arrowheads. There were, as well, several minerals, mined in the inland mountains, which could be made into the colorful body paints needed for religious ceremonies.

Southern tribes particularly wanted steatite from the Gabrielino tribe. Steatite, or soapstone, was a special metal which allowed heat to spread evenly through it. This made it a good choice to be used for cooking pots and flat frying pans. It could be carved into bowls because of its softness and could be decorated by carving designs into it. Steatite came from Catalina Island in the Coastal Gabrielino territory. Gabrielinos found steatite to be a fine trading item to offer for the acorns, deerskins, or obsidian stone they needed.

When people had no items to trade but needed something, they used small strings of shells for money. The small dentalium shells, which came from the far distant Northwest coast, had great value. Strings of dentalia usually served as money in the Northern California tribes, although some dentalia was used in the Central California tribes.

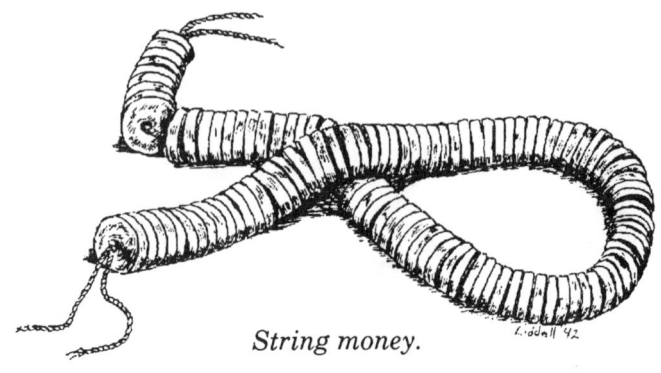

String money.

In southern California clam shells were broken and holes were bored through the center of each piece. Then the pieces were rounded and polished with sandstone and strung into strings for money. These were not thought to be as valuable as dentalia.

Strings of shell money were measured by tattoo marks on the trader's lower arm or hand.

Here is a sample of shell value:

A house, three strings
A fishing place, one to three strings
Land with acorn-bearing oak trees, one to five strings

A great deal of rock and stone was traded among the tribes for making tools. Arrows had to have sharp-edged stone for tips. The best stone for arrow tips was obsidian (volcanic glass) because, when hit properly, it broke off into flakes with very sharp edges. California tribes considered obsidian to be the most valuable rock for trading.

Some tribes had craftsmen who made knives with wooden handles and obsidian blades. Often the handles were decorated with carvings. Such knives were good for trading purposes. Stone mortars and pestles, used by the women for grinding grains into flour, were good trading items.

BASKETS & POTTERY

California tribal women made beautiful baskets. The Pomo and Chumash baskets, what few are left, show us that the women of those tribes might have been some of the finest basketmakers in the world. Baskets were used for gathering and storing food, for carrying babies, and even for hauling water. In emergencies, such as flooding waters, sometimes children, women, and tribal belongings crossed the swollen rivers and streams in huge, woven baskets! Baskets were so tightly woven that not a drop of water could leak from them.

Baskets also made fine cooking pots. Very hot rocks were taken from a fire and tossed around inside baskets with a looped tree branch until food in the basket was cooked.

Most baskets were made to do a certain job, but some baskets were designed for their beauty alone and were excellent for trading. Older women of a tribe would teach young girls how to weave baskets.

Pottery was not used by many California tribes. What little there was seems to have been made by those tribes living near to the Navaho and Mohave tribes of Arizona, and it shows their style. For example, pottery of the California tribes did not have much decoration and was usually a dull red color. Designs were few and always in yellow.

Ohlone hunter wearing deerskin camouflage.

Long thin coils of clay were laid one on top the other. Then the coils were smoothed between a wooden paddle and a small stone to shape the bowl. Pottery from California Native Americans has been described as light weight and brittle (easily broken), probably because of the kind of clay soil found in California.

HUNTING & FISHING

Tribal men spent much of their time making hunting and fishing tools. Bows and arrows were built with great care, to make them shoot as accurately as possible. Carelessly made hunting weapons caused fewer animals to be killed and people then had less food to eat.

Bows made by men of Southern California tribes were made long and narrow. In the northern part of the state bows were a little shorter, thinner, and wider than those of their northern neighbors. Size and thickness of bows depended on the size trees growing in a tribe's territory. The strongest bows were wrapped with sinew, the name given to animal tendons. Sinew is strong and elastic like a rubber band.

Arrows were made in many sizes and shapes, depending on their use. For hunting larger animals, a two-piece arrow was used. The front piece of the arrow shaft was made so that it would remain in the animal, even if the back part was

9

removed or broken off. The arrowhead, or point, was wrapped to the front piece of the shaft. This kind of arrow was also used in wars.

Young boys used a simple wooden arrow with the end sharpened to a point. With this they could hunt small animals like birds and rabbits. The older men of the tribe taught boys how to make their own arrows, how to aim properly, and how to repair broken weapons.

Tribal men spent many hours making and mending fishing nets. The string used in making nets often came from the fibers of plants. These fibers were twisted to make them strong and tough, then knotted into netting. Fences, or weirs, that had one small opening for fish, were built across streams. As the fish swam through the opening they would be caught in netting or harpooned by a waiting fisherman.

Hooks, if used at all, were cut from shells. Mostly hooks could be found when the men fished in large lakes or when catching trout in high mountain areas. Hooks were attached to heavy plant fiber string.

Dip nets, made of netting attached to branches that were bent into a circle, were used to catch fish swimming near shore. Dip nets had long handles so the fishermen could reach deep into the water.

Sometimes a mild poison was placed on the surface of shallow water. This confused the fish and caused them to float to the surface of the water, where they could be scooped up by a waiting fisherman. Not enough poison was used to make humans ill.

Not all fishing was done from the shore. California tribes used two kinds of boats when fishing. Canoes, dug out of one half a log, were useful for river fishing. These were square at each end, round on the bottom, and very heavy. Some of them were well-finished, often even having a carved seat in them.

Today we think of "balsa" as a very lightweight wood, but in Spanish, the word balsa means "raft". That is why Spanish explorers called the Native American canoes, made from tule reeds, "balsa" boats.

Balsa boats were made of bundled tule reeds and were used throughout most of California. They made into safe, lightweight boats for lake and river use. Usually the balsa canoe had a long, tightly tied bundle of tule for the boat bottom and one bundle for each side of the canoe. The front of the canoe was higher than the back. Balsa boats could be steered with a pole or with a paddle, like a raft.

Men did most of the fishing, women were in charge of gathering grasses, seeds, and acorns for food. After the food was collected, it was either eaten right away or made ready for winter storage.

Except for a few southern groups, California tribes had permanent villages where they lived most of the year. They also had food-gathering places they returned to each year to collect acorns, salt, fish, and other foods not found near their villages.

FOOD

Many different kinds of plant food grew wild in California in the days before white people arrived. Berries and other plant foods grew in the mountains. Forests offered the local tribes everything from pine nuts to animals.

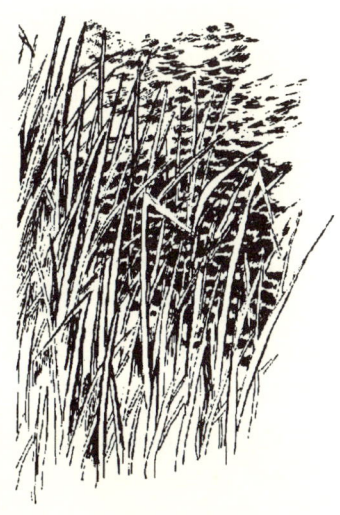

Native Americans found streams full of fish for much of the year. Inland fresh water lakes had large tule reeds growing along their shores. Tule could be eaten as food when plants were young and tender. More important, however, tule was used in making fabric for clothes and for building boats and houses. Tule was probably the most useful plant the California Native Americans found growing wild in their land.

Like all deserts, the one in southern California had little water or fish, but small animals and cactus plants made good food for the local tribes. They moved from place to place harvesting whatever was ripe. Tribal members always knew when and where to find the best food in their territory.

Acorns were the main source of food for all California tribes. Acorn flour was as important to the California Native Americans as wheat is to us today. Five types of California oak trees produced acorns that could be eaten. Those from black oak and tanbark oak seem to have been the favorite kinds.

Since some acorns tasted better than others, the tastiest ones were collected first. If harvest of the favorite acorn was poor some years, then less tasty acorns had to be eaten all winter long.

So important were acorns to California Indians that most tribes built their entire year around them. Acorn harvest marked the beginning of their calendar year. Winter was counted as so many months after acorn harvest, and summer was counted by the number of months before the next acorn harvest.

Acorn harvest ceremonies usually were the biggest events of the year. Most celebrations took place in mid-October and included dancing, feasts, games of chance, and reunions with relatives. Harvest festivals lasted for many days. They were a time of joy for everyone.

The annual acorn gathering lasted two to three weeks. Young boys climbed the oak trees to shake branches; some men used long poles to knock acorns to the ground. Women loaded the nuts into large cone-shaped burden baskets and carried them to a central place where they were put in the sun to dry.

Once the acorns were dried, the women carried them back to the tribe's permanent villages. There they lined special basket-like storage granaries with strong herbs to keep insects away, then stored the acorns inside. Granaries were placed on stilts to keep animals from getting into them and were kept beside tribal houses.

Preparing acorns for each meal was also the women's job. Shells were peeled by hitting the acorns with a stone hammer on an anvil (flat) stone. Meat from the nut was then laid on a stone mortar. A mortar was usually a large stone with a slight dip on its surface. Sometimes the mortar had a bottomless basket, called a hopper, glued to its top. This kept the acorn meat from sliding off the mortar as it was beaten. The meat was then pounded with a long stone pestle. Acorn flour was scraped away from the hopper's sides with a soaproot fiber brush during this process.

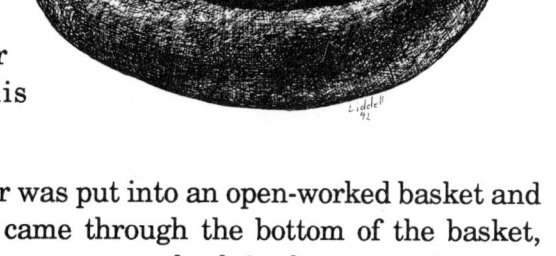

From there the flour was put into an open-worked basket and sifted. A fine flour came through the bottom of the basket, while the larger pieces were put back in the mortar for more pounding.

The most important process came after the acorn flour was sifted. Acorn flour has a very bitter-tasting tannin in it. This bitter taste was removed by a method called leaching. Many tribes leached the flour by first scooping out a hollow in sand near water. The hollow was lined with leaves to keep the flour from washing away. A great deal of hot water was poured through the flour to wash out (leach) the

13

bitterness. Sometimes the flour was put into a basket for the leaching process, instead of using sand and leaves.

Finally the acorn flour was ready to be cooked. To make mush, heated stones were placed in the basket with the flour. A looped tree branch or two long sticks were used to toss the hot rocks around so the basket would not burn. When the mush had boiled, it could be eaten. If the flour and water mixture was baked in an earthen oven, it became a kind of bread. Early explorers wrote that it was very tasty.

Historians have estimated that one family would eat from 1500 to 2000 pounds of acorn flour a year. One reason California native Americans did not have to plant seeds and raise crops was because there were so many acorns for them to harvest each year.

Whether they ate fish or shellfish or plant food or animal meat, nature supplied more than enough food for the Native Americans who lived in California long ago. Many believed their good fortune in having fine weather and plenty to eat came from being good to their gods.

RELIGION

Tribal members had strong beliefs in the power of spirits or gods around them. Each tribe was different, but all felt the importance of never making a spirit angry with them. For that reason a celebration to thank the spirit-gods for treating them well, took place before each food gathering and before each hunting trip, and after each food harvest.

Usually spiritual powers were thought to belong to birds or animals. Most California tribespeople felt bears were very wicked and should not be eaten. But Coyote seems to have been a kind leader who helped them if they were in trouble, even though he seems to have been a bit naughty at times. Eagle was thought to be very powerful and good to native Americans. In some tribes, Eagle was almost as powerful as Sun.

Tribes placed importance on different gods, according to the tribe's needs. Rain gods were the most important spirits to desert tribes. Weather gods, who might bring less rain or warmer temperatures, were important to northern tribes. A great many groups felt there were gods for each of the winds: North, South, East and West. The four directions were usually included in their ceremonial dances and were used as part of the decorations on baskets, pots, and even tools.

Animals were not only worshipped and believed to be spirit-gods, like Deer or Antelope, but tribal members felt there was a personal animal guardian for each one of them. If a tribal member had a deer as guardian, then that person could never kill a deer or eat deer meat.

California Native Americans believed in life after death. This made them very respectful of death and very fearful of angering a dead person. Once someone died, the name of the dead person could never again be said aloud. Since it was easy to accidentally say a name aloud, the name was usually given to a new baby. Then the dead person would not become angry.

Shamans were thought to be the keepers of religious beliefs and to have the ability to talk directly to spirit-gods. It was the job of a village shaman to cure sick people, and to speak to the gods about the needs of the people. Some tribes had several kinds of shamans in one village. One shaman did curing, one scared off evil spirits, while another took care of hunters.

Not all shamans were nice, so people greatly feared their power. However, if shamans had no luck curing sick people or did not bring good luck in hunting, the people could kill them. Most shamans were men, but in a few tribes, women were doctors.

Most California tribal myths have been lost to history because they were spoken and never written down. The legends were told and retold on winter nights around the home fires. Sadly, these were forgotten after the missionaries brought Christianity to California and moved tribal members into the missions.

A few stories still remain, however. It is thought by historians that northwest California tribes were the only ones not to have a myth on how they were created. They did not feel that the world was made and prepared for human beings. Instead, their few remaining stories usually tell of mountain peaks or rivers in their own territory.

The central California tribes had creation stories of a great flood where there was only water on earth. They tell of how man was made from a bit of mud that a turtle brought up from the bottom of the water.

Many southwest tribes believed there was a time of no sky or water. They told of two clouds appearing which finally became Sky and Earth.

Throughout California, however, all tribes had myths that told of Eagle as the leader, Coyote as chief assistant, and of less powerful spirits like Falcon or Hawk.

Costumes for religious ceremonies often imitated these animals they worshipped or feared. Much time was spent in making the dance costumes as beautiful as possible. Red woodpecker feathers were so brilliant a color they were used to decorate religious headdresses, necklaces, or belts. Deerskin clothing was fringed so shell beads could be attached to each thin strip of leather.

Eagle feathers were felt to be the most sacred of religious objects. Sometimes they were made into whole robes.

Religious feather charm.

Usually, though, the feathers were used just for decorations. All these costumes were valuable to the people of each tribe. The village chief was in charge of taking care of the costumes, and there was terrible punishment for stealing them. Clothing worn everyday was not fancy like costuming for rituals.

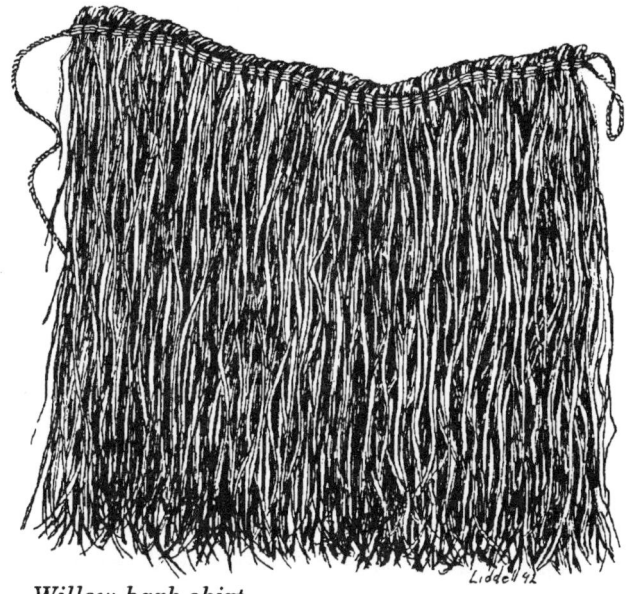

Willow bark skirt.

CLOTHING

Central and southern California's fine weather made regular clothes not really very important to the Native Americans. The children and men went naked most of the year, but most women wore a short apron-like skirt. These skirts were usually made in two pieces, front and back aprons, with fringes cut into the bottom edges. Often the skirt was made from the inner bark of trees, shredded and gathered on a cord. Sometimes the skirt was made from tule or grass.

In northern California and in rainy or windy weather elsewhere in the state, animal-skin blankets were worn by both men and women. They were used like a cape and wrapped around the body. Sometimes the cape was put over one shoulder and under the other arm, then tied in front. All kinds of skins were used; deer, otter, wildcat, but sea-otter fur was thought to be the best. If the skin was from a small animal, it was cut into strips and woven together into a fabric. At night the cape became a blanket to keep the person warm.

Because of the rainy weather in northern California, the women wore basket caps all the time. Women of the central and south tribes wore caps only when carrying heavy loads, where the forehead had to be used as support. Then a cap helped keep too much weight from being placed on the forehead.

Most California people went barefoot in their villages. For journeys into rough land, going to war, wood gathering, or in colder weather, the tribesmen in central and northwest California wore a one-piece soft shoe with no extra sole, which went high up on the leg.

Southern California tribespeople, however, wore sandals most of the time, wearing high, soled moccasins only when they traveled long distances or into the mountains. Leggings of skin were worn in snow, and moccasins were sometimes lined with grass for more comfort and warmth.

VILLAGE LIFE

Houses of the California tribes were made of materials found in their area. Usually they were round with domed roofs. Except for a few tribes, a house floor was dug into the earth a few feet. This was wise, for it made the home warmer in winter and cooler in summer. It also meant that less material was needed to make house walls.

Framework for the walls was made from bendable branches tied to support poles. Some frames of the houses were covered with earth and grass. Others were covered with large slabs of redwood or pine bark. Central California

Split-stick clapper, rhythm instrument. Hupa tribe.

villagers made large woven mats of tule reed to cover the tops and sides of houses. In the warmer southern area, brush and smaller pieces of bark were used for house walls.

Most California Native American villages had a building called a sweathouse, where the men could be found when they were not hunting, fishing or traveling. It was a very important place for the men, who used it rather like a clubhouse. They could sweat and then scrape themselves clean with curved ribs of deer. The sweathouse was smaller than a family house. Normally it had a center pole framework with a firepit on the ground next to the pole. When the fire was lit, some smoke was allowed to escape through a hole at the top of the roof; however, most was trapped inside the building. Smoke and heat were the main reasons for having a sweathouse. Both were believed to be a way to purify tribal members' bodies. Sweathouse walls were mainly hard-packed earth. The heat produced was not a steam heat but came from a wood-fed fire.

In the center of most villages was a large house that often had no walls, just a roof held up with poles. It was here that religious dances and rituals were held, or visitors were entertained.

Dances were enjoyed and were performed with great skill. Music, usually only rhythm instruments, accompanied the dances. For some reason California Native Americans did not use drums to create rhythms for their dances. Three different kinds of rattles were used by California tribes.

One type, split-clap sticks, created rhythm for dancing. These were usually a length of cane (a hollow stick) split in half lengthwise for about two-thirds of its length. The part still uncut was tightly wound with cord so it would not split all the way. The stick was held at the tied end in one hand and hit against the palm of the other hand to make its sound.

A pebble-filled moth cocoon made rhythm for shaman duties. These could range from calling on spirits to cure illnesses, to performing dances to bring rain. Probably the best sounds to beat rhythm for songs and dances came from bundles of deer hooves tied together on a stick. These rattles have a hollow, warm sound.

The only really "musical" instrument found in California was a flute made of reed that was played by blowing across the edge of one end. Melodies were not played on any of these instruments. Most North American Indians sang their songs rather than playing melodies on music instruments.

Special songs were sung for each event. There were songs for healing sick people, songs for success in hunting, war, or marriage. Women sang acorn-grinding songs and lullabies. Songs were sung in sorrow for the dead and during story-telling times. Group singing, with a leader, was the favorite kind of singing. Most songs were sung by all tribe members, but religious songs had to be sung by a special group. It was important that sacred songs not be changed through the years. If a mistake was made while singing sacred music, the singer could be punished, so only specially trained singers would sing ritual songs.

All songs were very short, some of them only 20 to 30 seconds long. They were made longer by repeating the melodies over and over, or by connecting several songs together. Songs usually told no story, just repeated words or phrases or syllables in patterns.

Song melodies used only one or two notes and harmony was never added. Perhaps that is why mission Indians, at those missions with musician priests, especially loved to sing harmony in the church choirs.

Songs and dances were good methods of passing rich tribal traditions on to the children. It was important to tribal adults that their children understand and love the tribe's heritage.

Children were truly wanted by parents in most tribes and new parents carefully watched their tiny babies day and night, to be sure they stayed warm and dry. Usually a newborn was strapped into a cradle and tied to the mother's back so she could continue to work, yet be near the baby at all times. In some tribes, older children took care of babies of cradle age during the day to give the mother time to do all her work, while grandmothers were often in charge of caring for toddlers.

Children were taught good behavior, traditions, and tribal rules from babyhood, although some tribes were stricter than others. Most of the time parents made their children obey. Young children could be lightly punished, but in many tribes those over six or seven years old were more severely punished if they did not follow the rules.

Just as children do today, Native American youngsters had childhood traditions they followed. For instance, one tribal tradition said that when a baby tooth came out, a child waited until dusk, faced the setting sun and threw the tooth to the west. There is no mention of a generous tooth fairy, however.

Tribal parents were worried that their offspring might not be strong and brave. Some tribes felt one way to make their children stronger was by forcing them to bathe in ice cold water, even in wintertime. Every once in a while, for example, Modoc children were awakened from sleep and taken to a cold lake or stream for a freezing bath.

But if freezing baths at night were hard on young Native Americans, their days were carefree and happy. Children were allowed to play all day, and some tribes felt children did not even have to come to dinner if they didn't want to. In those tribes, children could come to their houses to eat anytime of the day.

The games boys played are not too different from those played today. Swimming, hide and seek among the tule reeds, a form of tetherball with a mud ball tied to a pole, and willow-javelin throwing kept boys busy throughout the day.

Fathers made their sons small bows and arrows, so boys spent much time trying to improve their hunting skills. They practised shooting at frogs or chipmunks. The first animal any boy killed was not touched or eaten by him. Others would carry the kill home to be cooked and eaten by villagers. This tradition taught boys always to share food.

Another hunting tool for boys was a hollowed-out willow branch. This became like a modern day beanshooter, only the Native American boys shot juniper berries instead of beans. Slingshots made good hunting weapons, as well.

Girls and boys shared many games, but girls playing with each other had contests to see who could make a basket the fastest, or they played with dolls made of tule. Together, young boys and girls played a type of ring-around-the-rosie game, climbed mountains, or built mud houses.

As children grew older, the boys followed their fathers and the girls followed their mothers as the adults did their daily work. Children were not trained in the arts of hunting or basketmaking, however, until they became teenagers.

HISTORY

Spanish missionaries, led by Fray Junipero Serra, arrived in California in 1769 to build missions along the coast of California. By 1823, fifty years later, 21 missions had been founded. Almost all of them were very successful, and the Franciscan monks who ran them were proud of how many Native Americans became Christians.

However, all was not as the monks had planned it would be. Native American people had never been around the diseases European white men brought with them. As a result, they had no immunity to such illnesses as measles, small pox, or flu. Too many mission Indians died from white men's diseases.

Historians figure there were 300,000 Native Americans living in California before the missionaries came. The missions show records of 83,000 mission Indians during mission days. By the time the Mexicans took over the missions from the Spanish in 1834, only 20,000 remained alive.

The great California Gold Rush of 1849 was probably another big reason why many of the Native Americans died during that time. White men, staking their claim to tribal lands with gold upon it, thought nothing of killing any California tribesman who tried to keep and protect his territory. Fifty-thousand tribal members died from diseases, bullets, or starvation between the gold Rush Days and 1870. By 1910, only 17,000 California Indians remained.

Although the American government tried to set aside reservations (areas reserved for Native Americans), the land given to the Indians often was not good land. Worse yet, some of the land sacred to tribes, such as burial grounds, was taken over by white people and never given back.

Sadly, mission Indians, when they became Christians, forgot the proud heritage and beliefs they had followed for thousands of years. Many wonderful myths and songs they had passed from one generation to the next, on winter nights so long ago, have been lost forever.

Today some 100,000 people can claim California Native American ancestors, but few pure-blooded tribespeople remain. Our link with the Wanderers, who came from Asia so long ago, has been forever broken.

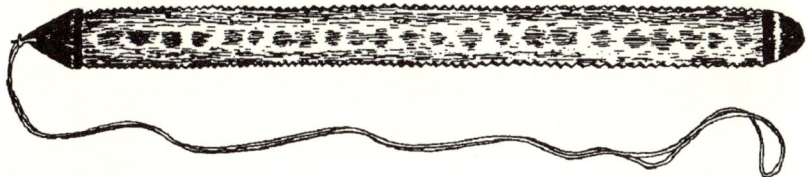

The bullroarer made a deep, loud sound when whirled above the player's head. Tipai tribe.

Villages were usually built beside a lake, stream, or river. Balsa canoes are on the shore. Tule reeds grow along the edge of the water and are drying on poles on the right side of the picture.

Women preparing food in baskets, sit on tule mats. Tule mats are being tied to the willow pole framework of a house being built by one of the men.

KAROK TRIBE

INTRODUCTION

The name Karok (Kaw' rock) comes from a Karok word *karuk,* meaning 'upstream.' This name has only been used since 1877, when White people spoke of the Karoks as being upstream from the Yurok tribe. Before that time the Karok tribe simply called itself 'people.' Both tribes lived along the shores of the Klamath River, the Yuroks living on the lower part of the river, close to where it enters the Pacific Ocean.

The Karok territory was found along middle segment of the Klamath River. On either side of the river the country was mostly mountainous. All the hunting, food gathering, and ceremonial sites (places) of the Karok people were in this mountain area of fir forests. Fishing for salmon and other types of fish was done in the many rivers and streams. There was plenty of food for everyone.

THE VILLAGES

The two kinds of buildings that made up Karok villages were dwelling houses, one for each family, and sweathouses. Both were in the shape of a rectangle and made of wooden planks. The tribe liked cedar planks best for house walls and roofs because it was not eaten by insects, nor did it rot as fast as other wood.

Planks were made by splitting logs with deer, elk, or antelope horns. Large rocks, called mauls, were used to pound one end of a horn against the wood, causing the logs to split. Stone adzes (cutting tools with thin, sharp blades) shaped the planks.

Floors of houses were dug into the ground several feet, leaving the roof as the main part of the house above ground. A stone-paved porch was built in front of each house.

Houses were entered by small, low doorways, so low that people had to crawl through them. A small doorway let in fewer cold winds during wintertime. Beneath the door was a plank ladder reaching to the floor below.

Inside the house was a stone-lined fire pit used for heating and for cooking. All meals were eaten there. Storage baskets and food-preparation tools and utensils were kept inside the houses. Clothing hung from framework poles and rafters.

Each village had several sweathouses, mainly because men used them for sleeping and weapon making and repairing, as well as for sweating. Men only went to their family houses for meals. Sweathouses were smaller in size than family dwellings but were built in the same style.

Usually, a sweathouse was only for men who were related to each other. These buildings were small so they could be more easily heated by the huge fires built in their central fire pits. A great deal of heat was needed to make bodies sweat. Sweating was the way tribal men purified their bodies. Body purifying was especially important before hunting and fishing trips. It was taboo for any woman, except women shamans, to enter a sweathouse.

There is no mention of assembly houses, which were found in almost all other California tribal villages.

Sweathouse of cedar planks. Floor is 3 to 4 feet below ground.

VILLAGE LIFE

An historian has described Karok people as being brave when they needed to be, very curious, quick to imitate others, and talkative and happy with fellow tribal members.

Their calendar year began on the shortest day (beginning of winter) and was divided into 13 months. They used a counting system based on units of 5 or 10, as we do today.

Owning objects and land was important to this tribe. Such things as dentalium shells (string money), woodpecker scalps, and obsidian arrow points and knife blades could make a Karok wealthy in the eyes of his fellow tribesmen.

Obsidian knife blade.

Those with wealth had a higher position in a village. As a result, tribal members were very thrifty so they could save money and become wealthy. They worked hard to do this. Strangely though, when villagers did become rich, it was considered bad manners to brag about how much money they had, for it might make poorer people wish them bad luck. Therefore, rich children were taught to treat poor people as equals.

In order to keep whatever positions they had earned in life, Karoks performed many rituals and obeyed all tribal laws so they would not lose their success by making spirits angry.

Even for gathering wood for the sweathouse, special rituals had to be followed. For instance, tall fir trees had to be cut from their uphill or downhill sides only, and hunters were to use pleading and prayers for success in hunting while they cut wood. Following tribal laws was important to Karok people.

There were no chiefs in Karok villages; rich men were the leaders. Village tribal members set up their own laws and rules to live by. There was no punishment given to those who disobeyed spiritual taboos; Karoks believed spirit-gods would punish a person who did something wrong, by giving that guilty villager bad luck in the future.

Those tribal members who committed crimes against others in their own village had to pay fines of money or property to the ones they had wronged. If criminals could not, or would not, repay a victim, they could be killed by that victim.

Every crime had its price. If a criminal paid all fines with money, even serious crimes like murder, the wrongdoer and the victims at once became friends again. A payment of shell money seemed to solve all legal problems of a village.

However, a poor criminal could sell himself into slavery if he committed a crime against a rich person and then did not have the money to pay his fine. Sometimes relatives could get together enough money to buy the criminal's freedom.

When a young man found a girl he wanted to marry, he visited the girl's father. The two men decided upon a price the young man would pay for his bride. The richer the girl's father, the more a bridegroom had to pay.

A newly-married couple went to the groom's parents' home to live. The wedding ceremony was simply an exchange of gifts between both

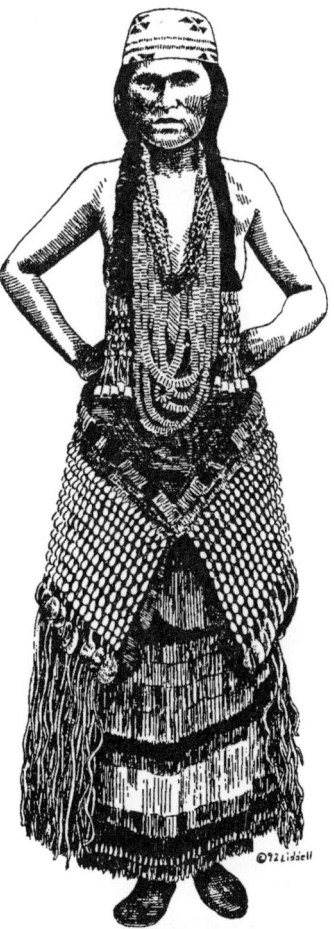

Wealthy woman wearing string bead necklace.

families. Later on, a groom might build his own dwelling near his father's home.

Sometimes a young man was thought to be a good mate for a woman, but he could not pay the bride price. Usually, he and his bride were allowed to marry but lived at her home, with the groom working for her father in order to pay off his debt.

Children were born in the dwelling house. They were given names when they were between one and three years of age. Until they married, girls remained with their mothers, learning how to gather and prepare foods, and make baskets and clothing. Boys moved to the sweathouse with their fathers at age three, so they could be trained in tribal laws and taught how to hunt and fish.

Boys received no ceremony when they became teenagers, but girls, at that age, were given a flower-dance ceremony. It always took place on a summer night, and adult men and women danced together at this celebration. Girls painted their faces for the dance and each carried a deerhoof rattle. Part of the ceremonial ritual was a training session where each girl was taught good tribal behavior, something she was to follow for the rest of her life.

When villagers died, other kinds of rituals were followed. A body was not allowed to be carried through the doorway of any house where the person died. One wall of such a house was taken apart and the corpse lifted through the hole. Later, a death house was purified with incense.

The body was taken to a family-owned grave plot near the home, where it was washed, and dentalium shells placed in its ears and nose. It was lowered into the grave with a rope, the head facing upstream. A fence was placed around the grave, and the dead person's belongings were hung on the fence and left there to rot.

The male relative chosen to be gravedigger remained at the grave for five days and nights. Karoks believed a body's ghost left for the 'afterworld-in-the-sky' only after haunting the dead person's village area for those five days.

What we call the Milky Way was called 'road of the dead' by villagers, since they thought it was this path that led to the afterworld. Leaders and rich people were believed to have their own, especially happy place in the afterworld. A dead person's name was not said aloud until it was 'recycled' by giving it to a child.

Myths were told around fires on long winter evenings. They usually had to do with life before humans lived upon the earth. Songs were included in the storytelling, and each myth usually ended with humans and animals arriving here on earth.

Myths and legends told of places and things close around tribal members. They recounted tales of sly, clever Coyote, who was not always good but was often the hero of Karok stories. Some myths were romantic and had love songs to go with them.

RELIGION

Religious rituals were mostly built around food and its importance to the tribe. Both men and women shamans were part of ritual ceremonies. Dancing, singing, feasting, and contests took place, along with the rituals.

Deer hoof rattle; handle is of vegetable fiber rope.

One large ceremony was held in the fall, at acorn harvest time. Another important ceremony happened in early spring when the first run of salmon began. The Deerskin dance and the Jumping Dance have been mentioned in tribal stories of ceremonies, but there are no descriptions of either dance.

Shamans were the spiritual leaders of any village. Shamans were thought to be supernatural, with the ability to tell the future and to talk to spirit-gods, but they were most needed as curing doctors.

Karok villages had two kinds of curing doctors. One was an herbal doctor who gave herb medicines to sick villagers. The second type of shaman was called a 'sucking' doctor. A sucking doctor's job was to search for "pain" in a sick person's body, and to remove it so the sick villager could get well.

This kind of doctor was like a magician, using sleight-of-hand tricks by pretending to suck out a 'pain object' from a patient. Symbols of pain could be anything from a small rock to a lizard or snake. A dance called the Brush Dance was often performed to cure a sick child. Some Brush Dances are still held today, most of them performed for tourists rather than to heal a youngster.

FOOD

Like most California tribes, Karok people lived by fishing, hunting wild animals, and gathering plant foods. Important river fish were salmon and eel. Salmon was roasted over a fire or dried in the sun and stored for winter food. Eel was usually fresh cooked and eaten right away.

Deer meat was eaten by Karoks more than any other large-animal meat. It was butchered in the woods and carried back to a village in a bundle. The spirits of deer were believed to go back to the hills after they died. Deer and elk were roasted over the open flame or hot coals of a fire. Sometimes meat was cooked in an earthen oven, a stone-lined pit with hot stones placed on top of the food.

Karoks also ate the meat of several different small animals, including rabbits and squirrels. However, the list of foods the tribal members did not eat was almost as long as the list of those they did eat. Karok people never ate coyotes, wolves, foxes, wildcats, gopher moles, bats, eagles, hawk vultures, crows, ravens, owls, meadowlarks, snakes, lizards, frogs, grasshoppers, or caterpillars.

Another tribal law did not allow them to eat bear meat and fresh salmon together. No reason is given for such a long list of food taboos, but the reason might have been religious.

The most important tribal plant food was the acorn, especially ones from the tanbark oak tree. The way acorns were prepared for cooking is explained on page 12 of Chapter One in this book.

Karok women made acorn soup from dough, prepared by grinding up nutmeats to which water was added. This was boiled in a cooking basket by tossing hot stones with the dough and water until the mixture was cooked. Acorn dough could also be baked into a hard bread by cooking it in an earthen oven.

Usually acorns were shelled and ground in mortars every day, as they were needed. Some Karok women, however, buried whole acorns in wet sand. By leaving the acorns buried for over a year, their bitter tannic acid taste would go away. In this method, acorns were boiled with the shells still on. After cooking them, acorn shells could be cracked with the teeth.

Sometimes wild-grass seeds were gathered in seed-beater baskets and heated with hot coals in basket trays. This method of cooking was called parching. Many other seeds could be cooked this way. Often seeds were ground into meal with a mortar and pestle. From this seed flour, bread or mush could be made.

Other nuts, bulbs or plant roots, and some plant leaves were eaten. Salt for seasoning came from salt deposit areas, places of ancient dried-up salt water lakes found in Karok territory, or by trading with coastal tribes to get seaweed.

HUNTING AND FISHING

Hunters always held a ceremonial ritual before going on a hunting trip. It included going without certain foods and treating their weapons with herbal incense. These rituals were an important way of making sure the supernatural gods would be pleased with the hunters. They did not want to take a chance on making spirit-gods angry just before a hunt.

When hunting in groups, Karok hunters used trained dogs to run deer into nooses, made of vegetable fiber, which caught and held large animals by the neck or foot until hunters could arrive to kill them with bows and arrows. Sometimes snares were used instead of nooses. Both nooses and snares were set along the sides of animal trails leading to favorite watering holes.

Another way of group hunting was to herd elk or deer into narrow ravines, using dogs or several villagers to help with the herding. Hunters, with spears and bows and arrows, waited at the opposite entrance to the ravine, killing the animals as they tried to run through.

A single hunter often wore a deerhead on his own head, throwing a deer skin around his shoulders at the same time. This way a hunter could stalk a deer and get close enough to more easily hit the animal with his arrows.

Bears were hunted in the winter while they were hibernating in caves. Hunters would first shout at a bear to come out, then drag the sleepy animal out of the cave to kill it. Bear meat was greasy, but there was enough of it to feed many people. Bear skins were made into warm blankets and capes.

Smaller animals, like squirrels and rabbits, could be caught in traps made of twigs and netting. Birds were also caught in snares and traps. Groundhogs and other animals who lived in the ground were sometimes smoked out of their holes.

Fishing was done in rivers and streams. Most fishermen built wooden platforms by the side of water. From these platforms, they could hit fish with clubs, catch them with plunge nets, or spear them. Harpoons with removable points were excellent weapons with which to catch salmon. Spears and nets could be used when fishing for eels.

Netting was made of fiber taken from wild iris leaves. Men made the netting by scratching off the leaf pulp with their fingernails until only the fiber remained. The fiber was then braided or twisted into cord.

A plunge net was made by attaching netting to a bendable tree branch, tied together in an oval shape. Long handles were put on plunge nets so fish could be scooped out of deep water. Steelhead and trout were caught with these nets. Boats used in fishing were hollowed-out red-wood logs the Karoks received in trade with the Yurok tribe.

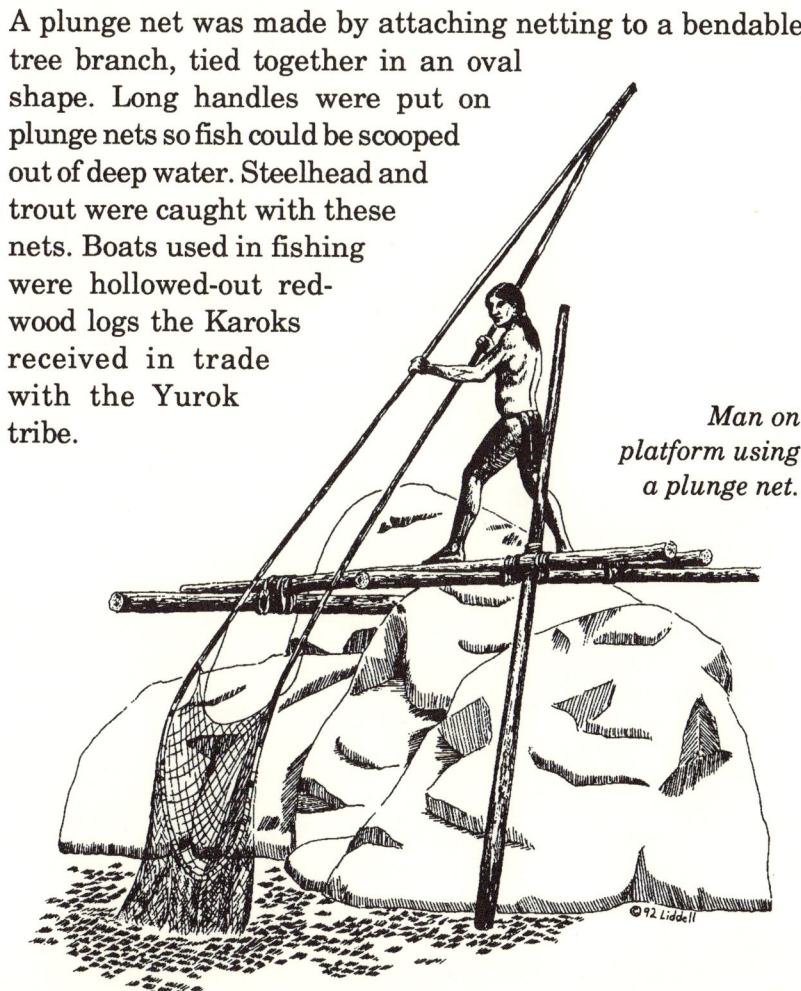

Man on platform using a plunge net.

BASKETS, WEAPONS, AND TOOLS

Baskets were the most important utensils made and used by Karok women. They were woven in all sizes and shapes, and were used for everything from baby cradles to storage, and from cooking pots and plates, to water carriers.

Hazelwood twigs and pine roots were the materials used to make Karok baskets. The ground beneath hazelwood trees was burned by the women so they could gather new tree sprouts which appeared after a fire. These young tree sprouts were exactly the right-size strands for making baskets. After being picked, and before being woven into baskets, the sprouts had to be peeled and dried in the sun.

Pine roots needed for basket materials were dug out of the ground, roasted under rocks placed beneath a fire. When cooked, the roots were split, dried, soaked, and scraped before they could be used. Bear lily and fern were used to sew design patterns on a basket.

Wood, stone, and fiber from plants provided most of what tribespeople needed for making tools and utensils. Sharp-edged stone tools were used to carve wood into storage boxes, to make spoons and stirring paddles for cooking, as well as small mortars and pestles for grinding herbs for medicine. These grinding tools were also needed to prepare grains, nuts, and other foods for meals.

Steatite, a soft, easy-to-carve rock mined for trade by the southern California Gabrielino tribe, was made into dishes to catch grease from cooking foods. Stone was used for mortars and pestles. Large stones served as hammers.

Meat was cut with obsidian (volcanic glass) knife blades, chipped into shape with the points of deerhorns, and attached to wooden handles. Obsidian was also excellent for arrow points. Men fashioned elkhorn into spoons for their own eating utensils.

The best bows were made of yew wood. Sinew (stretchy animal tendon) was either wrapped around, or glued to the backs of, most bows to make them more bendable. The more a bow could bend, the farther its arrows could go. Sinew was also used for the bowstring.

Arrows were made from syringa wood. If an arrow was to be shot at small animals, it was sharpened into a point at one end. The tip was then hardened by fire. Arrows needed for hunting large animals, or for warfare, had points carved out of obsidian attached to one end. A quiver made of small whole animal skins held each tribal man's arrows. Armor vests, worn as protection in battles, were made of strong elkhide or of small wooden rods tied together with fiber string.

Warrior with pole vest for protection in battle.

Thin, sharp splinters of animal bone made fine needles for sewing clothes and footwear. Bone or steatite was grooved to be used as arrow shaft straighteners. Wood sticks, sharpened at one end, were needed to start fires. A stick was twirled very rapidly between the palms of both hands, point side down, in a hollowed-out board. When friction heat built up enough, wood shavings placed in the hollow would begin to burn, thus starting the fire.

Elk, antelope, and especially deer were valuable to Karoks, not only for food, but for the many other things they provided tribal members. Nothing of a deer was wasted. A deer's hooves were made into ceremonial rattles, its tanned hide was used for clothing, and deer-leg tendons made fine elastic cord for binding objects together. An elk's large horns were used as wedges to split logs into wood planks for house walls.

CLOTHING

Because of the large number of animals found in their territory, a Karok woman made most of her family's clothing from animal hides. Buckskin, softened by tanning it with moss and animal brains, probably was the hide most often used.

Women's everyday clothing were two-piece apron skirts and deerskin capes. Hair was left on the cape's hide, which was worn around a woman's back and shoulders. The two-piece skirt, with the larger piece in back, was made of fringed buckskin and tied on at the waist. For special occasions, the front skirt panel was decorated with strings of digger-pine nuts and seashells.

In very cold weather, both men and women wore fur capes. Otherwise, men wore only a buckskin breechcloth or went without clothes. Children did not wear clothes for most of the year.

In this tribe, both women and men wore basket caps on their heads. Men wore their caps for special occasions. Women wore their hats more often and decorated them with fancy patterns. Basket hats were especially helpful to women when they carried heavy burden baskets on their backs.

A netting, or rawhide, tumpline was attached to one side of a burden basket. The tumpline went up across a woman's forehead, and then down to the basket's other side. This tumpline took some of the basket's tremendous weight off a woman's back by placing it onto her forehead. Basket caps were worn to keep pressure off the skin of the forehead.

The only time footwear was needed was if tribal members were going to travel through rough land. Then buckskin moccasins with thick elkskin soles were worn. If the land to be crossed had tall grass, hide leggings were worn, as well. Snowshoes made of hazelwood twigs and branches, with iris-cord webbing and buckskin ties, were worn when traveling over snow.

Ceremonial clothing was more colorful than everyday clothes. Maple-bark skirts were worn by women at ritual ceremonies. Shell necklaces and ear ornaments decorated the women's bodies.

A man's ceremonial costume was even more ornate. He wore a bright headband, and across his chest was draped a sash, or bandolier, decorated with brilliant red woodpecker scalp feathers. Face paint was made from soot, or red and white minerals mixed with oil. Men also wore pierced earrings and nose ornaments for festive events.

Both men and women let their hair grow long. Men wore theirs in a single ponytail, tied at the neck and hanging down the back. Women parted their hair in the middle, tying it at either shoulder with strips of buckskin or fur. Their ponytails hung in front of the shoulders.

Woman with basket cap.

Teenage girls' chins were tattooed with three vertical stripes. A sharp stone was used to cut the design into their skin. Soot and grease was put on the scratches.

GAMES

Storytelling helped to pass time throughout long, snowy winter evenings. The most popular free-time activities, however, were games of chance. Women liked one played with shells. Men filled free time indoors with a game which used several small sticks, one of which was marked with a ring around its middle. Players of one team hid the sticks behind their backs, while another team of men tried to guess which hand held the ringed stick.

Outdoor games were tough contests of athletic skills. One game using sticks, was described as being played with three-man teams. Players tried to throw two wooden blocks attached to a leather cord across a goal line.

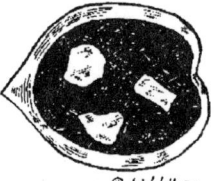

© Liddell 92

Dice made from walnut shells and filled with tar. Pieces of walnut shell added for decoration.

When playing indoors, children played hand games like cat's cradle. In warm weather, most of their free time was spent swimming, playing 'pretend,' or building with dirt.

HISTORY

The first White people to be seen by Karoks came in the early 1800s. They were Hudson Bay traders , coming from as far north as Canada to trap animals for their fur and hides. Fortunately, traders did not change Native American lifestyle very much. Then in 1850, gold miners invaded Karok territory, taking ownership of any land they thought had gold.

Gold miners considered tribal people as more of a bother than as the true owners of land they were destroying by digging for gold. White people burned down most of the Karok villages and ran Native Americans off their own land. Karok people fled to distant hills.

Settlers and gold miners built a town called Orleans on Karok land. When Karok people later returned to their territory, they found not only the town, but settlers' homes and farms where their villages and food gathering areas had been. Finally, in the late 1800s, the United States government gave Karoks permission to build their own houses on unused land near settlers' farms.

It was not until the mines ran out of gold that Karoks were left on their own. No reservations had been set aside for this tribe, so most of them moved into cities and towns near them, finding work as best they could. A few moved to reservations set aside in Shasta territory.

Population of the Karok tribe was thought to be 2,700 in 1848, before Europeans and American settlers arrived. During the gold rush, White people not only killed tribal members with guns, but their diseases of measles, small pox, and flu killed more Karoks than the weapons did. By 1930, only 755 tribal members were counted. In 1948, there were less than 25 full-blooded Karoks remaining, and all of them were old.

Times have changed. Being of Native American heritage has become a source of pride more than ever to tribal members, in recent years. Some ritual ceremonies have been brought back and are presented for tourists.

Many museums, including those of universities and colleges, are bringing the cultural life of Native Americans to all who visit them. Now that interest in Native American culture is growing, let us hope that more Karok beliefs will be researched and preserved.

KAROK TRIBE
OUTLINE

I. Introduction
    A. Meaning of name
    B. Territory

II. The villages
    A. Dwelling house description inside and outside
    B. Sweathouse description

III. Village life
    A. Personality of Karok people
    B. Knowledge
    C. Importance of wealth
    D. Tribal laws
    E. Crime and fines
        1. Slavery
    F. Marriage customs
    G. Childbirth customs
    H. Boys' childhood
    I. Girls' teenage ceremonies
    J. Death and mourning customs
    K. Myths and legends

IV. Religion
    A. Ritual ceremonies
    B. Shamans and curing

V. Food
    A. Meat eaten
    B. Meat not eaten
    C. Plant foods
        1. Acorns and seeds
        2. Roots and bulbs

VI. Hunting and fishing
    A. Hunting
        1. Rituals
        2. Group hunting
        3. Single hunters
        4. Bears
        5. Smaller animals

B. Fishing
  1. Platform fishing
  2. Nets. kinds and uses
  3. Boats
VII. Baskets, weapons, and other tools
  A. Baskets
  B. Wood tools
  C. Stone tools
  D. Bone tools
VIII. Clothing
  A. Tanning hides
  B. Women's
  C. Men and children's
  D. Basket caps
  E. Footwear
  F. Ceremonial costumes
  G. Hair styles and tattoos
IX. Games
  A. Storytelling and inside games
  B. Outside games
X. History
  A. First visit from white people
  B. Gold miners
  C. Settlers
  D. Population of tribe then and now
  E. Today

GLOSSARY

AWL: a sharp, pointed tool used for making small holes in leather or wood

CEREMONY: a meeting of people to perform formal rituals for a special reason; like an awards ceremony to hand out trophies to those who earned honors

CHERT: rock which can be chipped off, or flaked, into pieces with sharp edges

COILED: a way of weaving baskets which looks like the basket is made of rope coils woven together

DIAMETER: the length of a straight line through the center of a circle

DOWN: soft, fluffy feathers

DROUGHT: a long period of time without water

DWELLING: a building where people live

FLETCHING: attaching feathers to the back end of an arrow to make the arrow travel in a straight line

GILL NET: a flat net hanging vertically in water to catch fish by their heads and gills

GRANARIES: basket-type storehouses for grains and nuts

HERITAGE: something passed down to people from their long-ago relatives

LEACHING: washing away a bitter taste by pouring water through foods like acorn meal

MORTAR: flat surface of wood or stone used for the grinding of grains or herbs with a pestle

PARCHING:	to toast or shrivel with dry heat
PESTLE:	a small stone club used to mash, pound, or grind in a mortar
PINOLE:	flour made from ground corn
INDIAN RESERVATION:	land set aside for Native Americans by the United States government
RITUAL:	a ceremony that is always performed the same way
SEINE NET:	a net which hangs vertically in the water, encircling and trapping fish when it is pulled together
SHAMAN:	tribal religious men or women who use magic to cure illness and speak to spirit-gods
SINEW:	stretchy animal tendons
STEATITE:	a soft stone (soapstone) mined on Catalina Island by the Gabrielino tribe; used for cooking pots and bowls
TABOO:	something a person is forbidden to do
TERRITORY:	land owned by someone or by a group of people
TRADITION:	the handing down of customs, rituals, and belief, by word of mouth or example, from generation to generation
TREE PITCH:	a sticky substance found on evergreen tree bark
TWINING:	a method of weaving baskets by twisting fibers, rather than coiling them around a support fiber

NATIVE AMERICAN WORDS
WE KNOW AND USE

PLANTS AND TREES
hickory
pecan
yucca
mesquite
saguaro

ANIMALS
caribou
chipmunk
cougar
jaguar
opossum
moose

STATES
Dakota – friend
Ohio – good river
Minnesota – waters that
    reflect the sky
Oregon – beautiful water
Nebraska – flat water
Arizona
Texas

FOODS
avocado
hominy
maize (corn)
persimmon
tapioca
succotash

GEOGRAPHY
bayou – marshy body of
    water
savannah – grassy plain
pasadena – valley

WEATHER
blizzard
Chinook (warm, dry wind)

FURNITURE
hammock

HOUSE
wigwam
wickiup
tepee
igloo

INVENTIONS
toboggan

BOATS
canoe
kayak

OTHER WORDS
caucus – group meeting
mugwump – loner politician
squaw – woman
papoose – baby

CLOTHING
moccasin
parka
mukluk – slipper
poncho

BIBLIOGRAPHY

Cressman, L. S. *Prehistory of the Far West.* Salt Lake City, Utah: University of Utah Press, 1977.

Geiger, Maynard, O.F.M., Ph.D. *The Indians of Mission Santa Barbara.* Santa Barbara, CA 93105: Franciscan Fathers, 1986.

Heizer, Robert F., volume editor. *Handbook of North American Indians; California, volume 8.* Washington, D.C.: Smithsonian Institute, 1978.

Heizer, Robert F. and Elsasser, Albert B. *The Natural World of the California Indians.* Berkeley and Los Angeles, CA; London, England: University of California Press, 1980.

Heizer, Robert F. and Whipple, M.A.. *The California Indians.* Berkeley and Los Angeles, CA; London, England: University of California Press, 1971.

Heuser, Iva. *California Indians.* PO Box 352, Camino, CA 95709: Sierra Media Systems, 1977.

Macfarlen, Allen and Paulette. *Handbook of American Indian Games.* 31 E. 2nd Street, Mineola, N.Y. 11501: Dover Publications, 1985.

Murphey, Edith Van Allen. *Indian Uses of Native Plants.* 603 W. Perkins Street, Ukiah, CA 95482: Mendocino County Historical Society, © renewal, 1987.

National Geographic Society. *The World of American Indians.* Washington, DC: National Geographic Society reprint, 1989.

Tunis, Edwin. *Indians.* 2231 West 110th Street, Cleveland, OH: The World Publishing Company, 1959.

Credits:
Island Industries, Vashon Island, Washington 98070
Dona McAdam, Mac on the Hill, Seattle, Washington 98109

Acknowledgements:
Richard Buchen, Research Librarian, Braun Library,
Southwest Museum
Special thanks